THE STEAM TEAM Explains

Authors Steve Setford and Trent Kirkpatrick
Consultant Professor Robert Winston

Project editor Abby Aitcheson
Senior designer Jim Green
Editorial assistant Katie Lawrence
Designer Bettina Myklebust Stovne
Additional design Kanika Kalra Grover
US senior editor Shannon Beatty
US editor Margaret Parrish
Managing editor Jonathan Melmoth
Deputy managing art editor Ivy Sengupta
Managing art editor Diane Peyton Jones
DTP designers Sachin Gupta, Vijay Kandwal
Picture researcher Rituraj Singh
Jacket coordinator Issy Walsh
Jacket designer Elle Ward
Assistant pre-producer Abi Maxwell
Producer John Casey
Creative director Clare Baggaley
Publishing director Sarah Larter

Authors Steve Setford, Trent Kirkpatrick
Illustrator Mark Ruffle
Subject consultant Professor Robert Winston

First American Edition, 2020
Published in the United States by DK Publishing
1450 Broadway, Suite 801, New York, NY 10018

A catalog record for this book
is available from the Library of Congress.
ISBN 978-1-4654-9318-7

DK books are available at special discounts when
purchased in bulk for sales promotions, premiums,
fund-raising, or educational use. For details, contact:
DK Publishing Special Markets,
1450 Broadway, Suite 801, New York, NY 10018
SpecialSales@dk.com

Printed and bound in China

For the curious

www.dk.com

Contents

4 Foreword

6 Meet the Steam Team

8 Human body

10 Staying healthy

12 Food

14 Trees

16 Flowers and seeds

18 Animal groups

20 Insects

22 Food chains

24 Life cycles

26 Habitats

28 The environment

30 Seasons

32 Water

34 Rocks, soil, and fossils

36 The Earth and the moon

38 The sun

40 The planets

42 Patterns and symmetry

44 Time

46 Measuring

48 States of matter

50 Forces and motion

52 Magnets

54 Light

56 Sound

58 Color

60 Materials

62 Power

64 Electricity

66 Transportation

68 Computers and the Internet

70 Cities

72 Bridges and tunnels

74 Planes and rockets

76 Glossary

78 Index

80 Acknowledgments

Foreword

Of all the creatures on planet Earth, humans are the most creative. Our unique brain gives us imagination. Humans wish to find out, to explore, and to explain what puzzles us. This has led us to try to understand animals and plants, the other things around us, and how all this works. We call this science. However, humans are not merely fact-finders—we are excited by beauty, in what looks, smells, feels, and sounds good, or what seems interesting. Art, combined with science, also leads to us being creative, but we must be careful.

If we are not, so much of what we can make may damage Earth. This is why we need to understand science better. We have a duty to make sure we use our knowledge of life and what is around us responsibly. This book is a start to understanding life on our remarkable planet.

Robert Winston.

Professor Robert Winston

Meet the Steam Team

The Steam Team is here to explain fascinating facts about science, technology, engineering, art, and math.

Science
will help you ask the questions and discover the answers to explain how things work.

Technology
will show you how people use science to create new gadgets and machines.

Engineering
will teach you how science can be used to find and design solutions to problems.

Art
will help you to use your imagination and find out more about how art works.

Math
will teach you all about numbers, patterns, time, and more!

Human body

Bodies come in lots of different shapes and sizes, but all have the same basic parts. Some of these body parts we can see on the outside, but most are hidden under the skin.

Arms and **hands** let you pick up, carry, and throw things.

Hair keeps you warm or cool.

Eyes collect light for seeing.

Ears funnel in sounds for hearing.

Your **nose** breathes in air that goes to your lungs.

Your **mouth** sends food to your stomach.

Legs and feet get you from place to place.

Five senses

Your senses make you aware of the world around you. **Nerves** in your body send signals to your brain so it can figure out what's going on.

Sight
Your eyes form images of objects and sense what colors things are.

Hearing
Your ears can detect whether sounds are loud or quiet, high or low.

Smell
Nerves inside your nose detect smells in the air—and your brain lets you know if they're nice or nasty!

Taste
Your tongue's taste buds sense whether food is sweet, sour, bitter, salty, or savory.

Touch
Nerves in your skin tell you if things are hot or cold, and what their texture is like when you feel them.

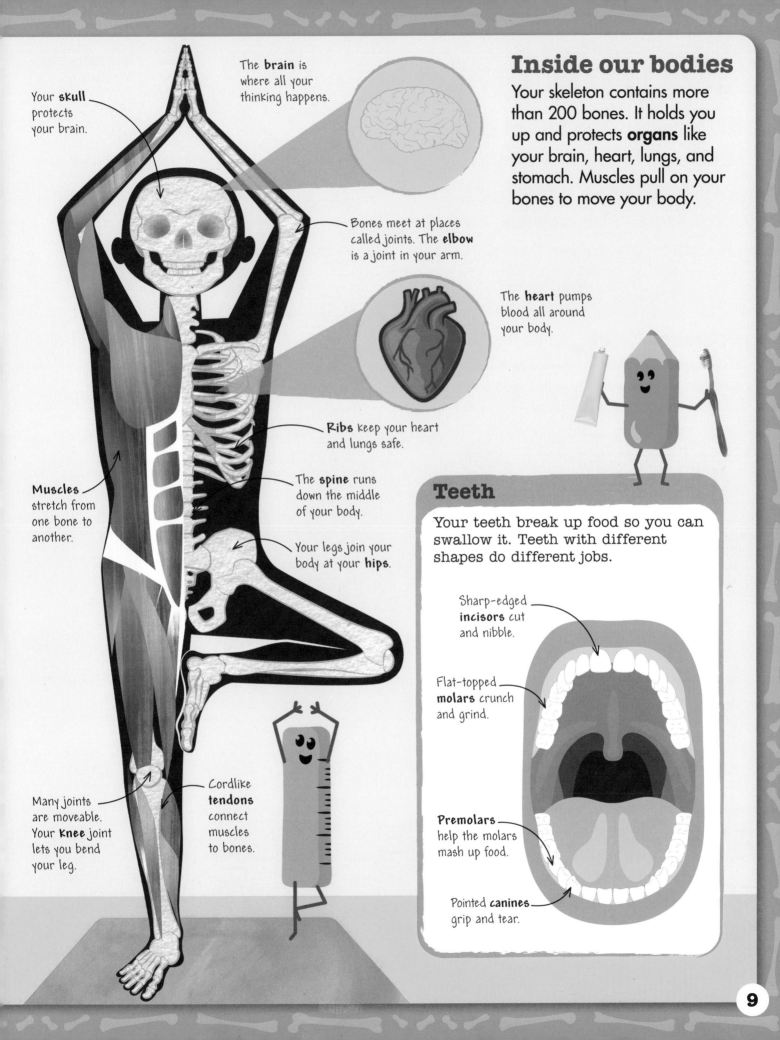

Inside our bodies

Your skeleton contains more than 200 bones. It holds you up and protects **organs** like your brain, heart, lungs, and stomach. Muscles pull on your bones to move your body.

Your **skull** protects your brain.

The **brain** is where all your thinking happens.

Bones meet at places called joints. The **elbow** is a joint in your arm.

The **heart** pumps blood all around your body.

Ribs keep your heart and lungs safe.

The **spine** runs down the middle of your body.

Muscles stretch from one bone to another.

Your legs join your body at your **hips**.

Many joints are moveable. Your **knee** joint lets you bend your leg.

Cordlike **tendons** connect muscles to bones.

Teeth

Your teeth break up food so you can swallow it. Teeth with different shapes do different jobs.

Sharp-edged **incisors** cut and nibble.

Flat-topped **molars** crunch and grind.

Premolars help the molars mash up food.

Pointed **canines** grip and tear.

Staying healthy

Your body is alive, and, like all life on Earth, it needs water and food to stay healthy. It also needs a good amount of sleep and exercise.

Seven-year-olds need about 10-and-a-half hours of sleep each night!

Sleep

For your body to function well, it needs to have enough time to rest. When we sleep, our bodies can repair themselves and grow.

Keeping clean

Brushing our teeth helps to stop tooth decay and gum disease, and washing our hands before eating stops us from spreading germs.

Brush your teeth after every meal.

Take a shower once a day.

Wash your hands before eating.

Healthy eating

A balanced diet is needed to stay healthy. It is important to eat a variety of foods from the five main food groups.

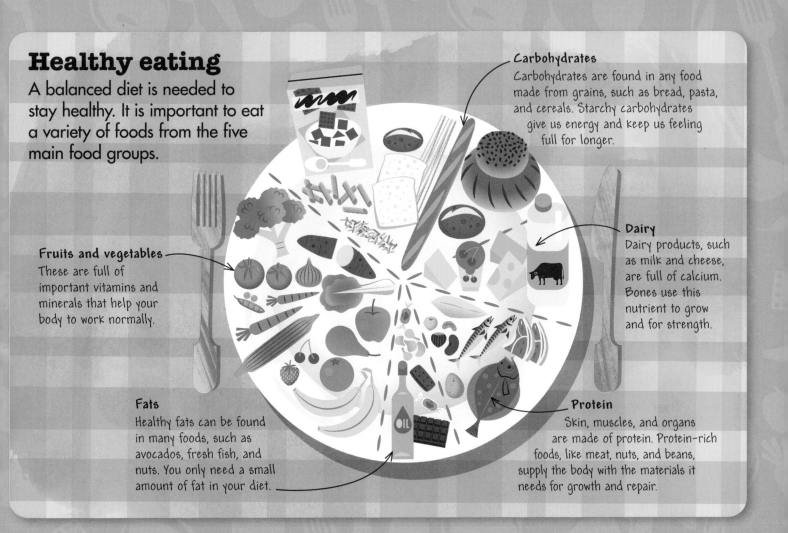

Carbohydrates
Carbohydrates are found in any food made from grains, such as bread, pasta, and cereals. Starchy carbohydrates give us energy and keep us feeling full for longer.

Dairy
Dairy products, such as milk and cheese, are full of calcium. Bones use this nutrient to grow and for strength.

Fruits and vegetables
These are full of important vitamins and minerals that help your body to work normally.

Fats
Healthy fats can be found in many foods, such as avocados, fresh fish, and nuts. You only need a small amount of fat in your diet.

Protein
Skin, muscles, and organs are made of protein. Protein-rich foods, like meat, nuts, and beans, supply the body with the materials it needs for growth and repair.

Weightlifting

Soccer

Gymnastics

Running

Cycling

There are many different ways to exercise and stay fit.

Being active

Our bodies need to be active to stay healthy. We need to work out to keep our muscles strong and our organs in tip-top shape.

Food

Almost all of our food comes from plants or animals, and it must be farmed, grown, or caught. Some food can be eaten right away, but other food must be changed, or **processed**, before you eat it.

Burger fixings

The meals we eat are usually a mixture of different foods. Let's unpack this tasty hamburger and see where the different foods inside it come from.

Cucumbers can be eaten raw or pickled to make pickles.

Patty
Patties can be made from many ingredients, including meat, vegetables, and beans. Meat comes from animals such as cows, pigs, and sheep.

Ketchup
Ketchup is made from processed tomatoes. First, the tomatoes are made into a paste. The paste is then cooked with sugar, vinegar, and other flavorings to form a rich sauce.

Lettuce
Farmers grow long rows of lettuce in fields or in big greenhouses. We use the green leaves in salads.

Tomato, a fruit

Onion, a vegetable

Cheese
Cheese can be made from the milk of cows, goats, sheep, and other animals.

Bun
Bread is made from wheat grown in fields. The wheat is ground down into flour. To make bread, the flour is mixed with ingredients such as salt, water, and yeast before being baked.

Farm machines

Tractors pull **plows** to dig up the soil. Then they pull machines called **seed drills** over the fields to sow seeds. When the crops are ripe, a **combine harvester** cuts and collects them.

Tractor and plow

Seed drill

Combine harvester

You can grow your own fruits and vegetables at home!

Trees

Trees are the largest plants on Earth. They can grow very tall and live for many years. Trees provide **wood**, which is used to make many things, including paper. Most trees are either **evergreen** or **deciduous**.

Photosynthesis

Trees and other plants make their own food through **photosynthesis**. They use sunlight, water from the soil, and **carbon dioxide** gas from the air to produce a sugar called glucose. They also give out **oxygen**, which we use to breathe.

Sunlight gives energy to the plant.

Carbon dioxide is absorbed by the leaves.

Oxygen is released into the air.

Water is taken in by the roots.

Green leaves
The leaves on evergreen trees remain green during the year.

Trunk
Trees have a strong stem called a **trunk**. It is covered with a thick, rough skin called **bark**.

Evergreen

These trees have leaves all year round. They can grow in either extremely hot or cold temperatures. A pine is one example of an **evergreen** tree.

Deciduous

Trees that lose their leaves in winter and produce flowers in spring are called **deciduous** trees. They grow best when it is not too hot or cold. Oak trees are deciduous.

Color change
In the fall, the leaves on deciduous trees change from green to orange and brown.

Leaf shapes

Leaves come in many shapes and sizes. Some are long and thin, while others are large and flat.

Beech
These shiny, waxy leaves can grow to be up to 4 in (10 cm) long and 2 in (5 cm) wide.

Maple
Leaves on this tree are hand-shaped. They are wide and short and have jagged edges.

Ash
Some trees have compound leaves. This is when many smaller leaves are attached to the same stem.

Ginkgo
These fan-shaped leaves sometimes split apart slightly as they grow.

Palms are another type of tree. They are often found in hot countries.

Flowers

Most flowers have a similar basic structure. **Stamens** produce fine grains called **pollen**, and **carpels** produce **ovules**. Brightly colored petals attract insects, which transfer the pollen to **pollinate** new flowers.

Flower shapes

There are many different flower shapes and they all attract different insects. Some insects fit down long, narrow flowers, while others need big petals to land on.

Rosette

Dome

Regular

Bell-shaped

Cone-shaped

Inside a flower

If you look closely inside the petals of a flower, you can see the parts that produce seeds.

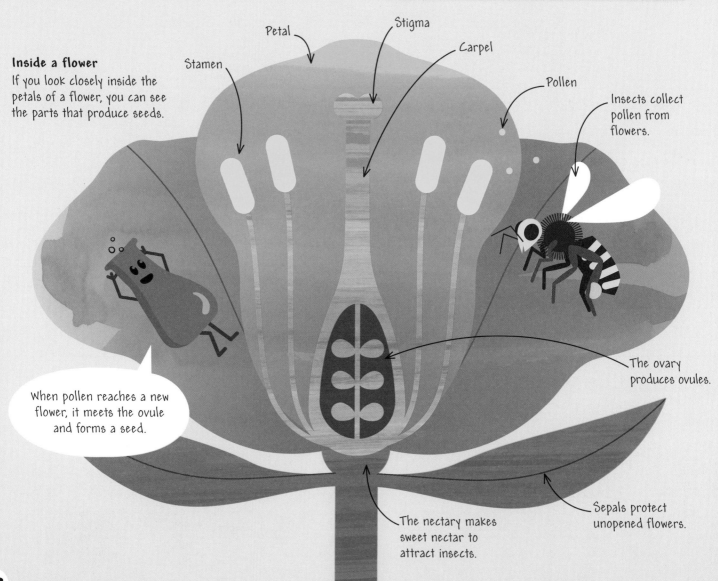

Petal

Stigma

Carpel

Stamen

Pollen

Insects collect pollen from flowers.

The ovary produces ovules.

When pollen reaches a new flower, it meets the ovule and forms a seed.

Sepals protect unopened flowers.

The nectary makes sweet nectar to attract insects.

Seeds

Many plants grow from seeds. In the right conditions, each seed can develop into a new plant. Seeds are spread to new places by the wind or by animals.

Dandelion seeds are feathery and light, so they can drift away on the breeze!

Seedling
If a seed gets enough rain and sunshine, it grows into a young plant called a seedling.

Flower
With help from the sun, the plant gets bigger. It grows more leaves and produces flowers. The colorful petals attract bees and other insects.

New seeds
The flowers form seeds. Some plants have seeds that blow away in the wind. Others hide their seeds in fruits. Animals eat them and spread the seeds in their droppings.

How do seeds grow?

Inside a seed is a tiny young plant called an embryo. If the embryo gets enough moisture, warmth, and nutrients, the seed will spring to life.

The seedling develops new leaves.

The baby stem grows upward and the root grows downward.

The seed is warm and moist in the soil.

Animal groups

Scientists have sorted, or **classified**, all animals into two categories. Animals with a backbone are called **vertebrates** and those without one are called **invertebrates**. These two main types can be divided into smaller animal groups.

Vertebrates

Animals with backbones come in many different shapes and sizes. Some animals live on dry land, while others live on or in water.

Birds
All birds have two wings, two feet, a beak, and feathers. However, not all birds can fly. Eagles are birds of prey.

Reptiles
This animal group has scaly skin. Reptiles lay eggs and are cold-blooded, which means they use sunlight to warm up their bodies. Snakes are reptiles.

Most mammals do not lay eggs. Instead, they give birth to live young and feed them milk.

Mammals
These animals are warm-blooded, which means they create heat inside their bodies. Mammals have hair or fur. This wolf is a type of mammal.

Amphibians
These vertebrates live near water so their bodies do not dry out. Amphibians lay their eggs in water. Frogs are amphibians.

Fish
Fish have gills for breathing underwater. They have slippery scales, fins, and a tail. Most fish lay eggs, but some give birth to live young. This yellow perch is a type of fish.

Invertebrates

There are many different types of invertebrate on Earth. They all have distinct features, but share one thing in common: they have no backbone.

Spiders

These eight-legged creatures can spin webs to catch prey to eat. Spiders are not insects—they belong to a group called arachnids.

Insects

All insects have six legs and three main body parts. This butterfly is a type of insect.

Worms

These invertebrates have long, soft bodies and often live under the ground in soil.

Crustaceans

Crustaceans, such as crabs, have a hard body covering, and most live in seawater. This crab has set up home in a seashell.

Mollusks

Mollusks have soft bodies. Many mollusks, such as snails, have a hard shell for protection, but others, including this octopus, don't. Most mollusks live in water.

Jellyfish

Jellyfish are invertebrates that live in water. They use their stinging tentacles to catch prey and pull it into their mouths.

Some worms, such as the black-and-yellow flatworm, live underwater!

Insects

There are billions of insects on Earth. They can be found almost anywhere. Most insects crawl or walk, and many can fly. Some can even swim underwater.

Body parts

All adult insects have three main body parts. These are the **head**, **abdomen**, and **thorax**. The bodies of young insects often look very different from their parents' bodies.

Types of insect

More than one million different **species**, or types, of insects have been discovered so far. Here are five of them.

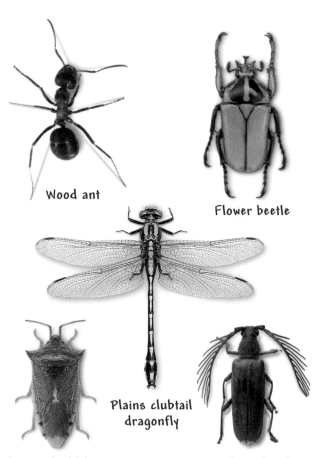

Wood ant

Flower beetle

Plains clubtail dragonfly

Green shield bug

Longhorn beetle

Abdomen
This body part holds an insect's stomach.

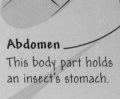

Butterflies have taste buds on their feet!

Antennae
Two antennae are
used for smelling.

Head
An insect's eyes
are found here.

Thorax
All six legs are
attached to the thorax.

Wings
Many insects have
wings, either one
or two pairs.

Legs

Insects have six **legs**. Each leg has
three **joints** that help it move in
different directions. Most baby insects
have tiny legs or no legs at all.

Skeletons

Insects and many other
invertebrates have a skeleton on
the outside of their bodies. This is
called an **exoskeleton**. Like a suit
of armor, it protects the body
from damage. Humans and other
animals have **endoskeletons**,
which means the skeleton is
inside their bodies.

Exoskeleton

Endoskeleton

Food chains

Each plant and animal depends on other living things around it to survive. Some animals eat plants, and others eat other animals. Nutrients from droppings and rotting material go into the soil and are used by plants.

Who eats what?

All animals are split into four categories, based on what they eat. These are **decomposers**, **omnivores**, **herbivores**, and **carnivores**.

Animals that eat only plants are called herbivores. Energy passes from plants to the animals that eat them.

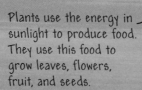

The sun is at the start of this food chain. Sunlight is the main source of energy for plants.

Plants use the energy in sunlight to produce food. They use this food to grow leaves, flowers, fruit, and seeds.

Apex predator

An **apex predator** is at the top of every food chain. Apex predators are powerful enough not to be eaten by any other animal. The grizzly bear and the great white shark are both apex predators.

Grizzly bear

Great white shark

Animals that hunt and eat other animals are called **predators**.

Decomposers eat plants and animals that have died. They recycle the energy from dead things back into the soil.

Omnivores can eat plants and animals. Chimps and humans are omnivores.

Herbivores eat only plants. Deer are herbivores.

Carnivores eat only animals, which they catch or hunt. Tigers are carnivores.

This shrew eats caterpillars. If there were too many caterpillars, there would be too few plants to feed them. The shrew is helping to keep the food chain in balance.

The apex predator in this food chain is an owl, which eats shrews. Energy has moved through the food chain from the sun all the way to the owl.

Animals that are hunted and eaten are called **prey**.

Life cycles

All livings things go through stages of growth.
Baby animals are born or hatch from eggs,
and new plants sprout from the soil. They grow,
become adults, and eventually have young of
their own. This is called a **life cycle**.

Human life cycle

Like all other animals, humans have a life cycle. Our
bodies change gradually as we journey through life,
slowly turning us from babies into **adults**.

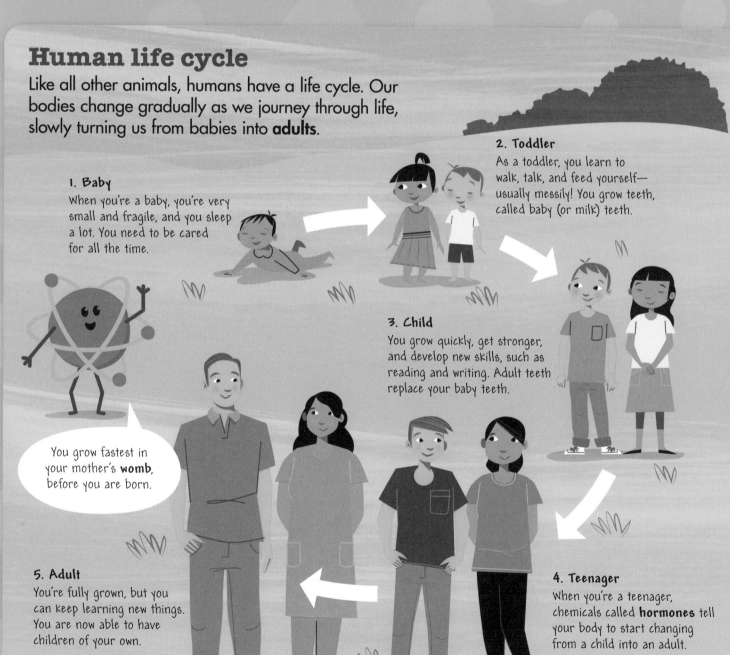

1. Baby
When you're a baby, you're very
small and fragile, and you sleep
a lot. You need to be cared
for all the time.

2. Toddler
As a toddler, you learn to
walk, talk, and feed yourself—
usually messily! You grow teeth,
called baby (or milk) teeth.

3. Child
You grow quickly, get stronger,
and develop new skills, such as
reading and writing. Adult teeth
replace your baby teeth.

4. Teenager
When you're a teenager,
chemicals called **hormones** tell
your body to start changing
from a child into an adult.

5. Adult
You're fully grown, but you
can keep learning new things.
You are now able to have
children of your own.

You grow fastest in
your mother's **womb**,
before you are born.

Frog life cycle

When frogs are born, they look completely different from their parents. They go through an amazing process of change, called **metamorphosis**, to prepare for adult life.

Almost all insects go through metamorphosis, too. That's how a caterpillar becomes a butterfly!

6. Adult frog
The full-grown frog spends most of its time on land, but it can still swim well. It returns to water to breed and lay its eggs.

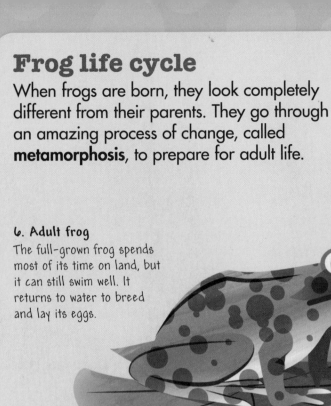

1. Eggs
Frogs lay clumps of eggs in ponds. The eggs have a thick coat of jelly to prevent them from being damaged.

5. Small frog
The young frog breathes air and it can now walk. It can leave the pond, but it stays in damp places on land.

2. Tadpoles
The eggs hatch into tadpoles. They have long tails for swimming and gills for breathing underwater.

4. Froglet
The front legs grow and the tail shrinks away. The tadpole is starting to look like a tiny frog.

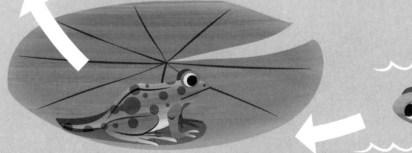

3. Developing legs
The tadpoles grow back legs. Their gills disappear, and they develop lungs to breathe air at the surface of the water.

Habitats

Habitats are areas where plants and animals live together, and where they find all the things they need to survive. Different habitats have different **climates**. Most animals and plants live only in one type of habitat.

Mountain

Plants grow close to the ground to avoid the cold wind. Birds can soar over the peaks, but ground animals must be **agile** to scramble over rocky slopes.

Forest

This habitat is full of shelter and food, so more animals live here than in any other land habitat. Some forests are hot and steamy, and others are cooler and drier.

Grassland

Where there's not enough rain, or the soil is too weak for most trees to grow, grass covers the land. Herds of grazing animals roam over these grasslands.

Deserts

It rarely rains in the desert. The plants and animals there have to survive on very little water and cope with boiling-hot days and very cold nights.

Thick fur on a camel's back shields its body from the hot sun.

Polar

The polar regions of the Arctic and Antarctic are snowy, icy places with freezing winds. Few plants grow there, so most animals are meat-eaters.

Thick fur and a layer of **blubber** (fat) keep polar bears dry and warm.

Ocean

Fish and many other sea creatures breathe underwater through **gills**. However, some marine animals, such as whales, must come to the surface for air.

Coral reefs are home to around one-third of all marine life.

The environment

The Earth's environment is the world around us, and it is home to all living things. It is made up of water, air, and land. Keeping all three of these things clean and healthy is essential for the survival of our planet.

Healthy environment

When water, air, and land are kept clean, the environment is healthy. Animals and plants have all the things they need to live and grow.

These trees are green and lush. They will keep releasing the oxygen we need to breathe.

Animals are healthy and have enough food to eat.

The river's water is clean and many fish live here.

Unhealthy environment

When we drop litter, cut down forests, pollute the skies with smoke, or pour waste into rivers, we hurt the plants and animals that live in these environments.

Factories and some power plants release harmful pollution into the air.

Trees, which take in unbreathable carbon dioxide, have been chopped down.

Trash can be very harmful to animals.

Plastic products do not break down naturally; they damage the environment.

What can we do?

We can do lots of things to help the environment, such as use less energy and water, plant trees, recycle things, and make laws to protect habitats and wildlife.

Switch off
Switching off lights, computers, and other devices when we leave a room saves energy. Then power plants don't need to produce as much electricity.

Recycle
It's better to reuse what we already have rather than buy new things. If we have to throw items away, we can recycle them. The materials they are made from can be turned into new products.

Save water
Water must be cleaned and made safe before we can use it, and that takes energy. Using less water saves energy.

Plant trees
Trees release oxygen, which our bodies take in as we breathe. Many forests are being cut down, so we need to plant lots of new trees to keep the air healthy.

Global warming

The polluting gases that we release into the air are heating up planet Earth. This is called global warming. It is harming the environment and melting the ice at the North and South poles. Many polar animals are struggling to survive.

What we do to help has an impact on people, plants, and animals everywhere!

Cycling
Bicycles do not produce polluting exhaust gases like cars do. So, when we travel by bike instead of car, we cause less air pollution.

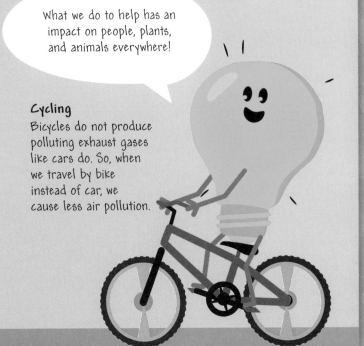

Seasons

Some parts of the world have **four seasons**: spring, summer, fall, and winter. Other places on Earth are always warm and have a dry and a wet season. Each season brings different **weather**.

Spring
In spring, the days start to become longer and warmer. More sunlight and rain help plants to grow. Spring is the season when plants and trees grow new flowers.

Winter
The coldest season also has the shortest days. Some trees are bare in winter, and there can be snowstorms and freezing temperatures.

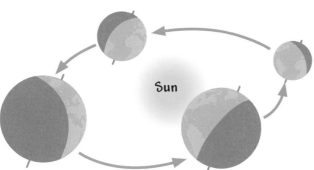

Sun

Why seasons happen
Earth is tilted as it travels around the sun. At different times of the year, some places get more sunlight as they lean toward the sun and then less sunlight as they lean away. This causes the seasons to happen.

Tropical seasons

Tropical regions are places where the weather is always warm. Some tropical regions have two seasons. The **wet season** has lots of rain and the **dry season** is very hot.

Dry season

Wet season

Summer

The season with the longest days and warmest weather is called summer. Plants grow tall and sprout delicious fruits, vegetables, or nuts.

Fall

Days start to get shorter in the fall, and the sun shines less. It becomes colder, and leaves on some trees lose their green color and fall off.

Some animals go to sleep for a long time (hibernate) or travel to warmer places during the fall and winter.

Water

The amount of water on Earth is always the same. It just gets recycled, or used again and again. There is **liquid water** in the sea, **water vapor** (gas) in the air, and **solid water** (ice) at the poles. All living things, including humans, need water to survive.

The sun's energy powers the water cycle.

Clouds release their water as rain, snow, or hail.

Water evaporates from the sea into the air, where it condenses and forms clouds.

The water cycle

The world's water is always moving between the sea, sky, and land. This nonstop recycling is known as the water cycle.

Water runs downhill in rivers or sinks into the ground.

The water returns to the sea.

Types of water

Almost all of Earth's water is salt water. The rest is fresh water, some of it frozen into ice.

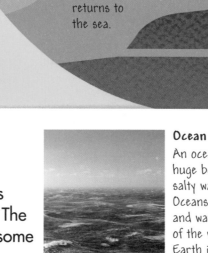

Ocean
An ocean is a huge body of salty water. Oceans have tides and waves. Most of the water on Earth is found in the oceans.

Lake
A lake is a large body of fairly still, fresh water surrounded by land. Rivers and streams may flow into or out of the lake.

Only a little of Earth's water is fresh water. It is a precious resource, so we must not waste it. Here are some ways to be more water-wise:

- Turn off the faucet when you're brushing your teeth.
- Take a shower instead of a bath.
- Tell an adult if you see a water leak.

Water makes up more than half your body's weight!

Washing
We use soap and water to clean ourselves. To keep germs away, we wash our hands before handling food and after going to the bathroom.

Laundry
To get rid of dirt and stains, washing machines churn and spin clothes around with water and a type of soap called detergent.

Cooking
We use water in the kitchen to boil and steam food. Then we use more water to wash dishes.

Swimming
Splashing and swimming in a pool is fun, and it's good exercise, too! Special chemicals are added to pool water to kill germs.

Drinking
We lose water when we breathe, sweat, pee, and poop. To stay healthy, we need to drink plenty of water each day to replace what we lose.

River
Rivers flow from hills and mountains to lower land, getting bigger along the way. They wind across the land until they meet the sea.

Glacier
Glaciers are like rivers of ice that move downhill from high mountains. There are also huge sheets of ice in polar regions.

Rocks, soil, and fossils

The rocks that make up Earth's hard outer shell are often covered by soil, sand, ice, or water. Some contain fossils, which tell us about life on Earth long ago.

Rocks

Rocks are made of tiny crystals of natural substances called **minerals**. The main types of rock are called sedimentary, igneous, and metamorphic.

Sedimentary
This rock is made from sand, mud, or minerals from the shells and skeletons of sea creatures.

Igneous
This rock is formed when magma (hot, molten rock) cools and hardens.

Metamorphic
Rock that has been changed by heat and high pressure underground is called metamorphic.

Soil

Soil is the loose material that covers much of the land, and it's where plants grow. It's made of rotten material mixed with minerals and bits of broken rock.

There are more microbes in a teaspoon of soil than there are people on Earth!

Humus is the rotting remains of dead plants and animals.

Topsoil is a mixture of minerals and humus. Many plant roots grow here.

Subsoil is rich in minerals. It has less humus than topsoil.

This layer is mostly made of large rock pieces. Plant roots don't reach this far.

Under the soil layers is solid rock called **bedrock**.

Fossils

Fossils are the remains of ancient animals and plants preserved in rock. They were buried by sand or mud and turned to stone over millions of years.

Paleontologist
Paleontologists use fossils to find out what plants, animals, and other living things were like in the past.

Paleontologists use special tools to dig up, or excavate, fossils.

Fossils are found when the rock above wears away.

Fossils are dug up carefully, so they aren't damaged.

Sometimes a whole fossil skeleton is found.

Dinosaurs

Dinosaurs were spectacular reptiles that ruled Earth from 245 to 66 million years ago. Dinosaur fossils include bones, teeth, eggs, footprints, and even poop!

Skull of Iguanodon

T. rex's scary teeth were up to 12 in (30 cm) long!

Tyrannosaurus rex skeleton

Fossilized egg of Oviraptor

The Earth

Our home, the planet Earth, has a hard, rocky shell, a middle of softer rock, and a core of metal. It's all wrapped up in a mixture of gases called the atmosphere.

Sustaining life

Earth has everything that living things need to survive. These are water, oxygen, energy from the sun, and soil, which provides the raw materials needed for plant growth.

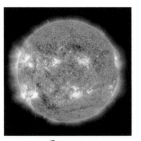

Energy

Oxygen

Water

Soil

The atmosphere is mostly made up of the gases nitrogen and oxygen.

More than two-thirds of Earth's surface is covered by water.

Much of Earth's rocky land is covered by soil and green plants.

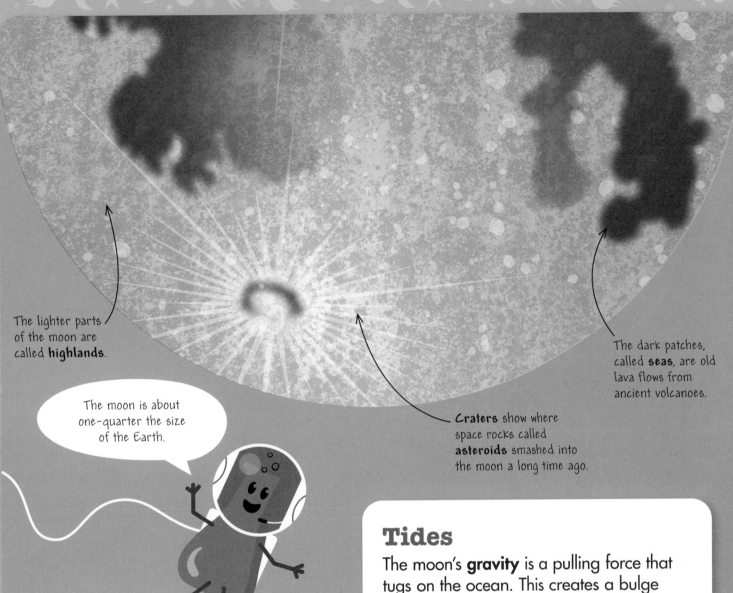

The lighter parts of the moon are called **highlands**.

Craters show where space rocks called **asteroids** smashed into the moon a long time ago.

The dark patches, called **seas**, are old lava flows from ancient volcanoes.

The moon is about one-quarter the size of the Earth.

The moon

The moon is a dry, dusty, airless world. It **orbits**, or travels around, Earth as the pair whiz around the sun. The moon looks bright in the night sky because it reflects light from the sun.

Tides

The moon's **gravity** is a pulling force that tugs on the ocean. This creates a bulge in the sea on either side of the Earth. We call these bulges high tides. As Earth spins, the tides move around the planet.

The ocean also bulges on the opposite side of the Earth.

The ocean bulges where the moon's gravity is strongest.

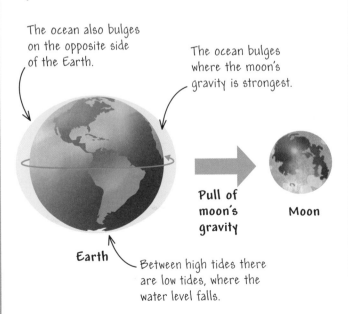

Pull of moon's gravity

Moon

Earth

Between high tides there are low tides, where the water level falls.

The sun

At the center of the solar system is a star we call the sun. It is a vast ball of hot, glowing gases that are held together by a force called **gravity**. The sun is made up of many layers. It has been shining for nearly 5 billion years.

Core
At the heart of the sun is the core, which produces the sun's energy. It's a bit like a giant furnace, with hydrogen gas as the fuel that keeps it burning.

How hot?

The sun's surface is extremely hot, about 9,600°F (5,300°C). In its core, however, temperatures soar to a mind-boggling 29 million°F (16 million°C).

Moving sun

The sun appears to travel across the sky each day, but it's really the Earth that is moving. Earth spins on its axis, but we don't notice this movement. So it seems to us as though the sun is moving instead.

Inner layers
Energy from the core moves very slowly through the sun's layers. It can take more than 100,000 years to reach the surface!

Atmosphere
The sun's atmosphere stretches for thousands of miles into space.

Sunspots
Dark blotches called sunspots are cooler parts of the surface.

Surface
The sun's surface **emits**, or gives off, huge amounts of light, heat, and other energy, which travel out into space. Some of it reaches Earth.

Solar eclipse
When the moon briefly passes between the sun and the Earth, it casts a shadow on Earth. We call this a **solar eclipse**. Sometimes, the sun's light is completely blocked by the moon's shadow. For a few minutes, day seems like night!

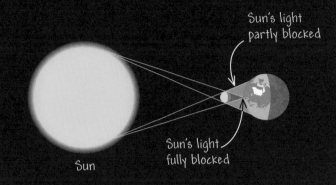

Sun's light partly blocked

Sun's light fully blocked

Sun

The sun's future
About 5 billion years from now, the sun will run out of fuel. It will swell up and its outer layers will blow away. Only the core will be left, which will slowly cool and fade away.

Light from the sun takes just over eight minutes to get to Earth.

Never look directly at the sun with the naked eye or through binoculars—bright sun can damage your eyes!

Mercury
Mercury is the smallest planet, and it is closest to the sun. It is covered in craters.

Venus
This planet is almost as big as the Earth. It is the hottest planet, with a thick **atmosphere** that traps heat. It also has clouds that rain sulfuric acid!

Earth
Our planet, Earth, is a special place. It's the only planet with oceans of water, plenty of oxygen in its atmosphere, and living things.

Astronomers have found planets around other stars in deep space. Some may be able to support life.

The planets

Earth is one of eight planets that orbit, or go around, the sun in our solar system. Mercury, Venus, Earth, and Mars are rocky planets. Jupiter, Saturn, Uranus, and Neptune are giant planets made mostly of gas.

Saturn
The second-largest planet, Saturn, has beautiful rings made up of pieces of ice and rock. Saturn has 82 moons—poor old Mercury has none.

Planet parade
As the planets whiz around the sun, they're held in place by the sun's **gravity**. The rocky planets are the closest to the sun.

The sun

Mercury

Venus

Earth

Mars

Mars is a cold desert world with a thin atmosphere. It's called the Red Planet because iron in the soil gives it a rusty red color.

Jupiter

The largest planet, Jupiter, is covered with bright bands of swirling cloud. The red spot on its surface is a huge storm as big as the Earth!

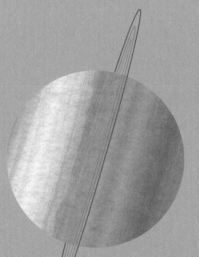

Uranus

The other planets spin upright as they orbit the sun, but Uranus spins on its side. Scientists think the clouds on Uranus smell like rotten eggs!

Neptune

Cold, bright-blue Neptune has the strongest winds. Frozen clouds scoot around the planet at more than 1,200 mph (2,000 kph).

Dwarf planets

Objects that are bigger than **asteroids** (lumps of rock and metal that orbit the sun) but smaller than the rocky planets are called dwarf planets. Most of them lie beyond Neptune.

Pluto

Pluto is the largest dwarf planet, but it's still only half as wide as the United States. When it snows on Pluto, the snow is red!

Ceres

The smallest dwarf planet, Ceres, lies in the asteroid belt between Mars and Jupiter. It has an ice volcano that erupts frozen lava.

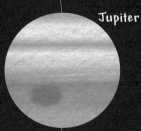

Mars

Jupiter

Saturn

Uranus

Neptune

Asteroid belt

Patterns

Patterns are repeating **sequences** of things, such as shapes. You can see patterns everywhere—on clothes, furniture, and also in nature.

Making patterns

We can make a simple pattern with just two shapes, repeating one after the other. Adding different shapes or changing the colors makes the pattern more complicated.

This pattern repeats a circle followed by a square.

The pattern here is star, triangle, yellow circle, green circle.

These shapes are in a random order—there is no pattern.

Tessellation

When a pattern is made of identical shapes that fit together without any gaps or overlaps, it is called **tessellation**. You can see tessellation here in the six-sided cells in a honeycomb.

Symmetry

There are two types of symmetry: reflective and rotational. We can see both types of symmetry in the world around us.

Rotational symmetry

A shape has **rotational symmetry** if it can be turned around at its center until it fits exactly into its original outline. Perfectly formed snowflakes have rotational symmetry.

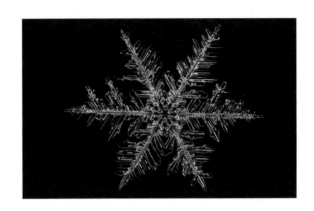

Reflective symmetry

A shape has reflective symmetry if you can draw a line through it and split it into two identical halves. Some shapes have no lines of symmetry, while others have many.

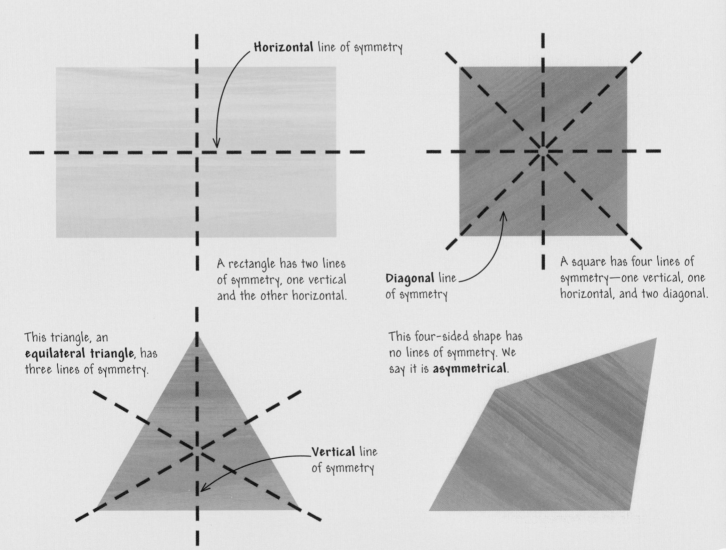

Horizontal line of symmetry

A rectangle has two lines of symmetry, one vertical and the other horizontal.

Diagonal line of symmetry

A square has four lines of symmetry—one vertical, one horizontal, and two diagonal.

This triangle, an **equilateral triangle**, has three lines of symmetry.

This four-sided shape has no lines of symmetry. We say it is **asymmetrical**.

Vertical line of symmetry

Time

We use clocks and watches to find out what time it is. Calendars help us keep track of the days, weeks, and months—and how long we have to wait for special occasions!

Clocks

Clocks measure time in **hours**, **minutes**, and **seconds**. There are 60 seconds in a minute, 60 minutes in an hour, and 24 hours in a day. Clocks can be **analog** or **digital**.

There are 1,440 minutes—or 86,400 seconds—in a day. Luckily, we have clocks to count them for us!

This hand shows the seconds. Not all clocks have this hand.

Digital clock
A **screen** shows the time in numbers. The numbers change as time passes. A 12-hour clock uses the numbers 1 to 12, and a 24-hour clock uses 00:00 to 23:59.

This number shows the hour.

A **colon** (two dots) separates the hour and minutes.

Analog clock
The clock **face** has the numbers 1 to 12 on it. Pointers called **hands** show the time by moving around the clock face and pointing to different numbers.

The shortest hand shows you the hour.

This hand points to the minutes. It is longer than the hour hand.

This number shows the minutes. It's 15 minutes past 10.

Calendar

There are usually 365 days in a year, divided into **12 months**: January, February, March, April, May, June, July, August, September, October, November, and December.

Sunday is one of the seven days of the week.

October is the tenth month of the year.

This calendar is for the year 2026.

OCTOBER 2026

Sun	Mon	Tue	Weds	Thurs	Fri	Sat
				1	2	3
4	5	6	7	8 *My birthday!*	9	10
11	12	13	14	15	16	17
18	19	20	21	22	23	24
25	26	27	28	29	30	31

There are about four weeks in each month.

Months range from 28 to 31 days long. October lasts for 31 days.

Every fourth year is 366 days long, instead of 365. We call this a **leap year**. The extra day is added to February.

Length

We can measure how long, wide, and tall things are with rulers and tape measures. They measure in inches, feet, and yards (imperial) or millimeters, centimeters, and meters (metric).

This side measures in inches.

Ruler
Most rulers show 12 inches on one side and 30 centimeters on the other.

This side measures in centimeters.

There are 10 millimeters in one centimeter and 100 centimeters in one meter.

This scale shows degrees Celsius (°C).

This scale shows degrees Fahrenheit (°F).

The liquid moves up the tube as the temperature rises.

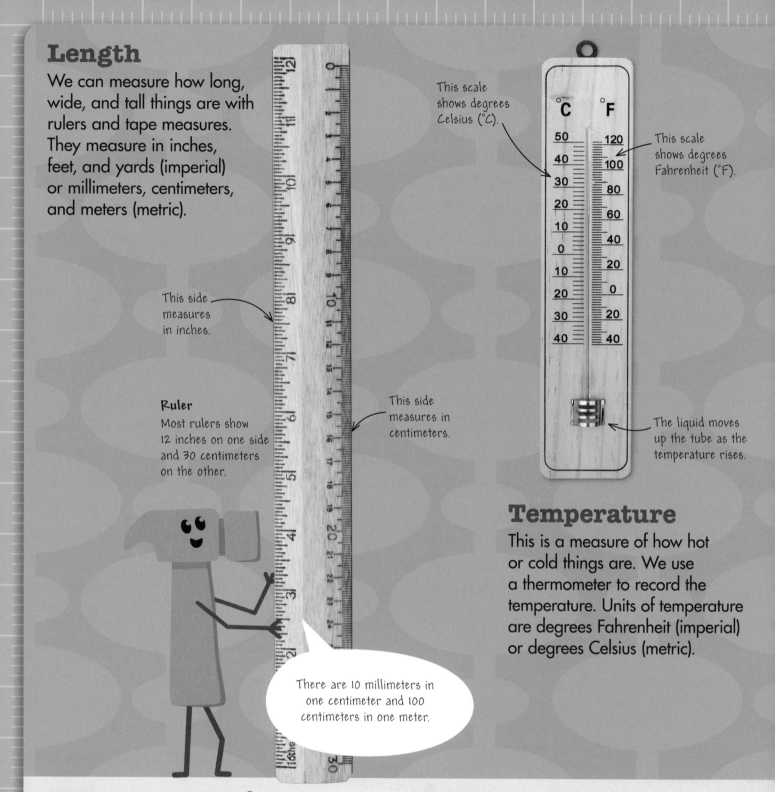

Temperature

This is a measure of how hot or cold things are. We use a thermometer to record the temperature. Units of temperature are degrees Fahrenheit (imperial) or degrees Celsius (metric).

Measuring

Measurements help us build, cook, shop, describe the weather, and much more. We use different units to measure things. The two main measurement systems are called **imperial** and **metric**.

Volume

Volume is the size of an object in three dimensions—length, width, and height. It tells you how much space something takes up.

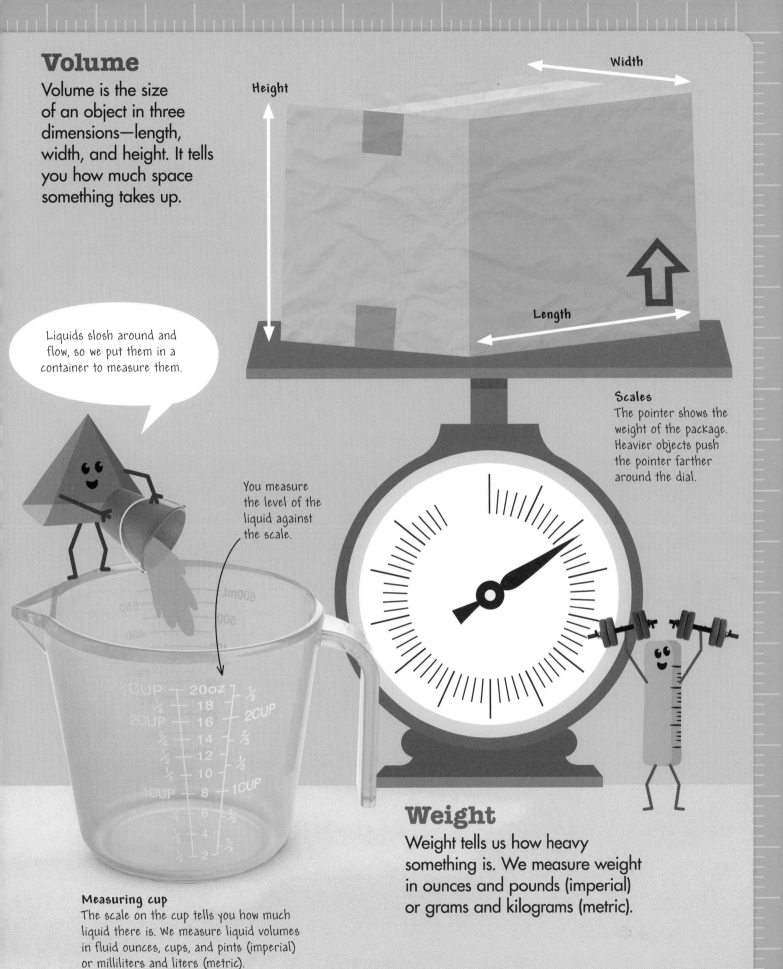

Height

Width

Length

Liquids slosh around and flow, so we put them in a container to measure them.

You measure the level of the liquid against the scale.

Scales
The pointer shows the weight of the package. Heavier objects push the pointer farther around the dial.

Measuring cup
The scale on the cup tells you how much liquid there is. We measure liquid volumes in fluid ounces, cups, and pints (imperial) or milliliters and liters (metric).

Weight

Weight tells us how heavy something is. We measure weight in ounces and pounds (imperial) or grams and kilograms (metric).

States of matter

Everything on Earth is made of tiny parts, or **particles**, of matter. The three main states of matter are **solid**, **liquid**, and **gas**. The particles in each state behave in different ways. Matter can change from one state to another.

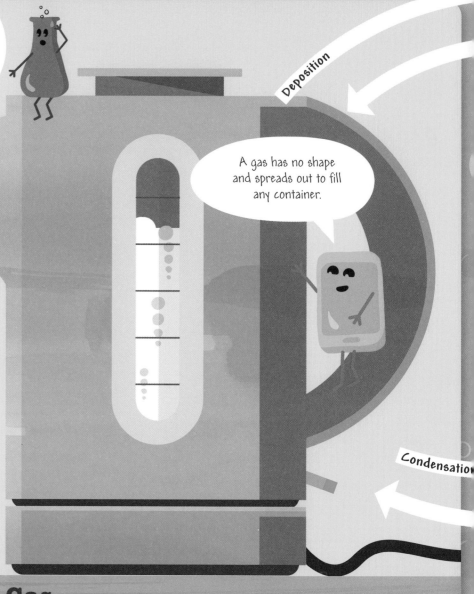

When water is boiled, it gets so hot that some of it turns into water vapor.

Deposition

A gas has no shape and spreads out to fill any container.

Condensation

Matter magic

Water vapor is invisible, but it is in the air all around us. When it cools, it condenses into water droplets as clouds, fog, or rain.

Water vapor condenses on cold windows.

Gas

When liquid water is heated to a high enough temperature, it turns into a gas. This gas is called water vapor. A gas becomes a solid in a process called **deposition** and a liquid in a process called **condensation**.

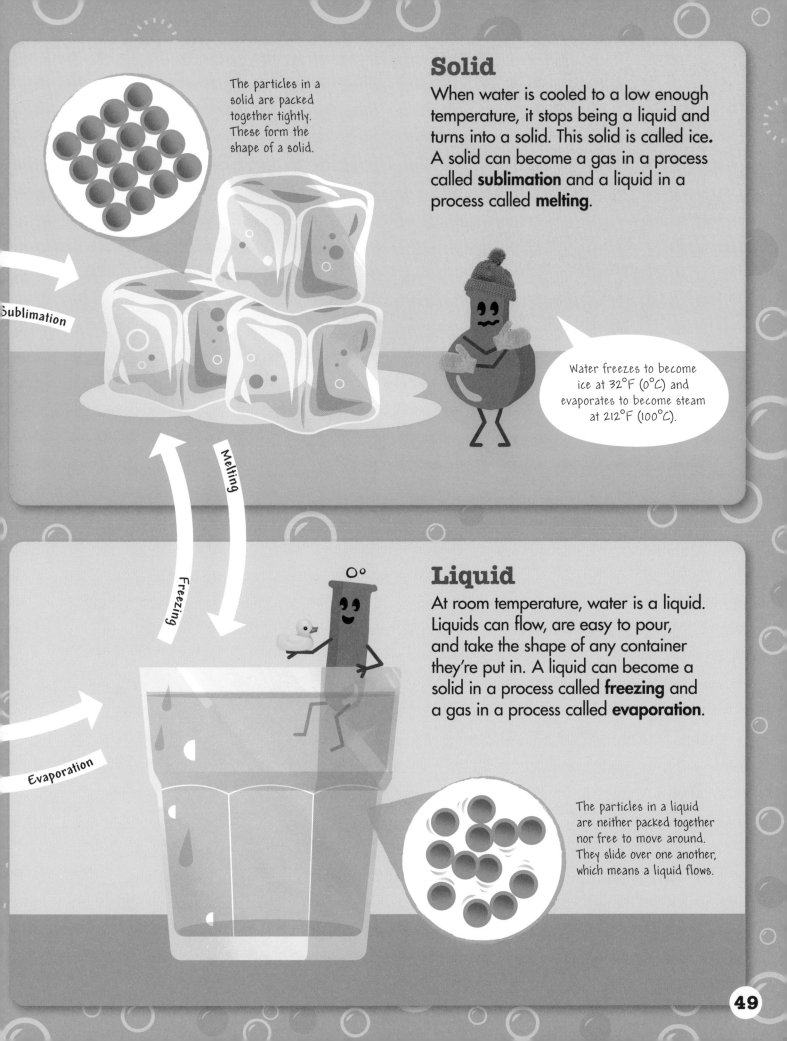

The particles in a solid are packed together tightly. These form the shape of a solid.

Sublimation

Melting

Freezing

Evaporation

Solid

When water is cooled to a low enough temperature, it stops being a liquid and turns into a solid. This solid is called ice. A solid can become a gas in a process called **sublimation** and a liquid in a process called **melting**.

Water freezes to become ice at 32°F (0°C) and evaporates to become steam at 212°F (100°C).

Liquid

At room temperature, water is a liquid. Liquids can flow, are easy to pour, and take the shape of any container they're put in. A liquid can become a solid in a process called **freezing** and a gas in a process called **evaporation**.

The particles in a liquid are neither packed together nor free to move around. They slide over one another, which means a liquid flows.

49

Forces and motion

A **force** is a push or a pull that makes an object start or stop moving, speed up or slow down, or change direction. When forces combine, they can hold things still or **balance** them.

This rocket's engine burns fuel to produce thrust.

Push

When you kick a ball, your foot pushes the ball and it shoots off. Engines in vehicles produce a force called **thrust**, which pushes the vehicles along.

As the car speeds up, it gains more kinetic energy.

Thrust
Rockets produce so much thrust that they can fly away from Earth and hurtle into space.

Kinetic energy
A moving object, such as this car, has a type of energy called **kinetic energy**. The faster the object is moving, the more kinetic energy it has.

Balanced forces

These tug-of-war teams are pulling with equal force in opposite directions. The forces are balanced and cancel each other out, so neither team moves.

Unless one team pulls more strongly than the other, the ribbon stays over the line.

Pull

Pulls also make things move. The harder you pull, the faster an object travels. When you throw a ball into the air, a pulling force called **gravity** makes it fall to the ground.

Without the pull of Earth's gravity, if this apple broke off from its branch, it would drift off through the air!

A scientist named Isaac Newton discovered gravity in 1666, when an apple landed on his head!

Gravity
Gravity is a pulling force between all objects. Bigger objects have more gravity. Planets, such as Earth, have really strong gravity.

We only notice air when the wind blows!

Friction

When one surface moves over another, a sneaky force called **friction** tries to slow it down. The rougher the surfaces, the more friction between them.

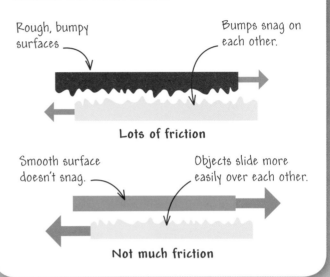

Rough, bumpy surfaces

Bumps snag on each other.

Lots of friction

Smooth surface doesn't snag.

Objects slide more easily over each other.

Not much friction

Air resistance
A force called air resistance acts on things moving through air. It tries to resist the pull of gravity on falling objects. That's why a parachute drifts safely down to the ground.

Magnets

A magnet can push and pull objects without even touching them. It does this using an invisible force called magnetism, which is strongest at the two ends, or **poles**, of the magnet. Magnets only affect **magnetic materials**, such as iron, nickel, cobalt, and steel.

The two poles of a magnet are called its north (N) and south (S) poles. A curved magnet like this is known as a horseshoe magnet.

N

Is it magnetic?

Metals that contain iron are magnetic and will be attracted to a magnet. Other materials that do not contain iron, including most metals, will not be affected by a magnet.

This plastic pen is not magnetic, so it's not attracted to the magnet.

This rubber does not contain magnetic material. It is not affected by the horseshoe magnet.

This steel ruler is magnetic because it contains iron, which is attracted to the magnet.

How strong are magnets?

Magnets can be incredibly strong. Some are so powerful that they can lift up very heavy items, such as cars.

This crane is using a magnet to lift heavy scrap metal.

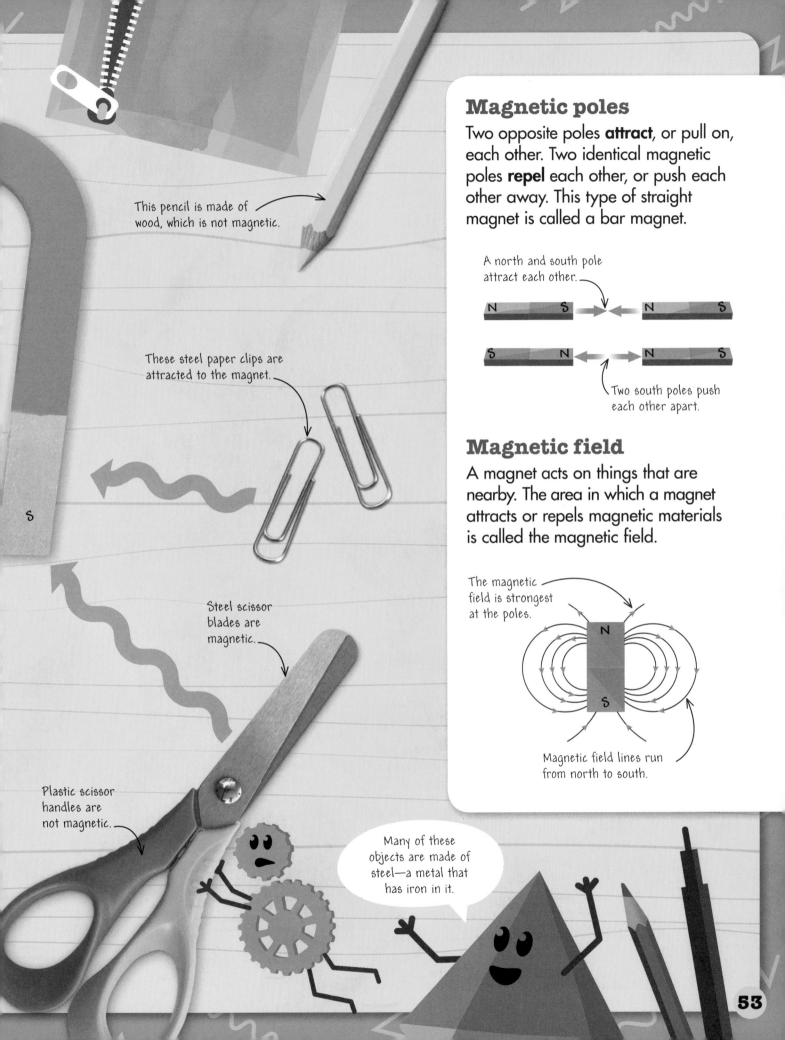

This pencil is made of wood, which is not magnetic.

These steel paper clips are attracted to the magnet.

Steel scissor blades are magnetic.

Plastic scissor handles are not magnetic.

S

Many of these objects are made of steel—a metal that has iron in it.

Magnetic poles

Two opposite poles **attract**, or pull on, each other. Two identical magnetic poles **repel** each other, or push each other away. This type of straight magnet is called a bar magnet.

A north and south pole attract each other.

N   S   →←   N   S

S   N   ←→   N   S

Two south poles push each other apart.

Magnetic field

A magnet acts on things that are nearby. The area in which a magnet attracts or repels magnetic materials is called the magnetic field.

The magnetic field is strongest at the poles.

N

S

Magnetic field lines run from north to south.

Light

Light is a type of energy that we can detect with our eyes. It is made up of tiny traveling waves. Light looks white, but it is really made up of lots of different colors combined.

Light source
A light source is anything that sends out light. The sun, stars, candles, lamps, car headlights, and fireflies are all light sources.

Rays
Light travels in straight lines called rays. You have probably seen rays of light streaming through a window on a sunny morning.

Bouncing light

Light rays can bounce, or **reflect**, off things and change direction. This is how we see things. Light from a source, such as a lamp or flashlight, hits an object and reflects into our eyes.

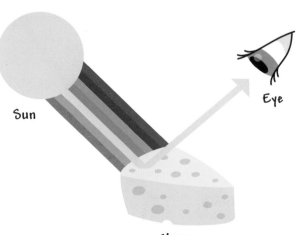

Sun

Eye

Cheese

Wavelengths

We see can the different colors in light when water droplets in the sky split sunshine into a rainbow. Some colors of light have longer waves, others have shorter waves.

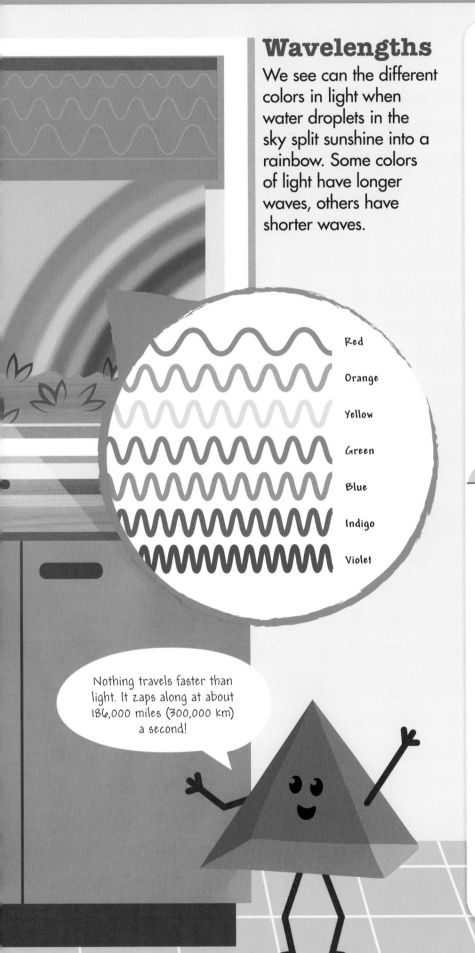

Red

Orange

Yellow

Green

Blue

Indigo

Violet

Nothing travels faster than light. It zaps along at about 186,000 miles (300,000 km) a second!

Shadows

If light is blocked by an object, a dark area called a shadow forms. A shadow's shape and size depend on the position of the light source.

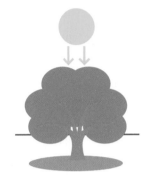

High
In the middle of the day, when the sun is high in the sky, the tree has a short shadow.

Low
Near sunrise and sunset, when the sun sits lower in the sky, the tree's shadow gets longer.

In front
When the sun is in front of the tree, the shadow forms behind the tree.

Behind
When the sun is behind the tree, the shadow is cast in front of the tree.

Sound

Sound is a form of energy produced when objects vibrate, or move rapidly to and fro. The vibrations, called sound waves, spread out through the surrounding air.

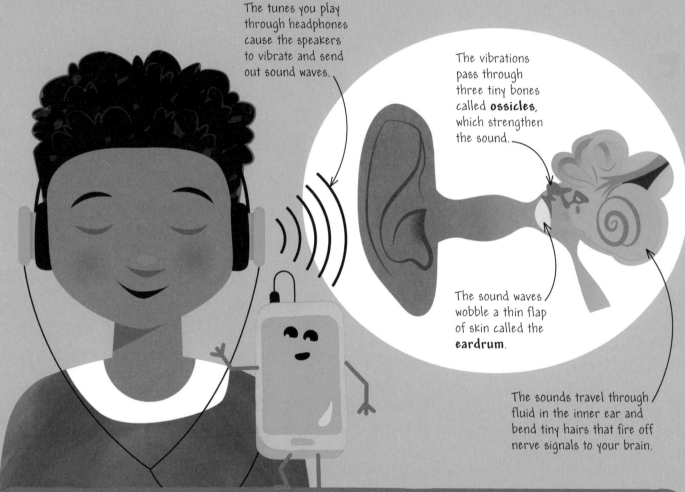

The tunes you play through headphones cause the speakers to vibrate and send out sound waves.

The vibrations pass through three tiny bones called **ossicles**, which strengthen the sound.

The sound waves wobble a thin flap of skin called the **eardrum**.

The sounds travel through fluid in the inner ear and bend tiny hairs that fire off nerve signals to your brain.

Sound travels

Sound needs a material to move through, such as wood, metal, brick, air, or water. In air, sounds travel at 1,080 ft (330 m) a second, but they travel more than four times faster in water.

Echoes
Shout "Hello!" in a cave, and the word bounces off the cave walls and comes back to your ears. The sound that bounces back is an echo.

Water
Sounds travel farther, as well as faster, in water than in air. Humpback whales call to each other with "songs" that can be heard 100 miles (160 km) away.

Making music

Music is sounds called notes arranged in a particular order or pattern. There are five main families of musical instruments.

Woodwind

Blowing into a woodwind instrument causes the air inside to vibrate and make a sound.

Percussion

You strike or shake percussion instruments to make them vibrate.

Keyboards

Keyboards can play many notes at once. Pressing a piano key makes a hammer inside strike a string.

String

You pluck the strings of a guitar or harp to play notes. To play a violin, you move a bow over the strings so they vibrate.

Brass

A brass instrument is a long tube bent into coils. You blow into the mouthpiece to play different notes.

Melody is the tune, and it is made up of notes. Harmony is the sound of two or more notes played at once.

Color

Colors bring our world to life. You can mix just three colors—red, blue, and yellow—to make any other color! Red, blue, and yellow are called **primary colors**.

Yellow
Cheerful yellow brightens up our day. Yellow **dye** was once made using cow pee!

Orange
Orange, yellow, and red are said to be warm colors. They remind us of sunshine, summer, and warm fires.

Secondary colors

When you mix two primary colors, you get a secondary color. Orange, green, and purple are **secondary colors**.

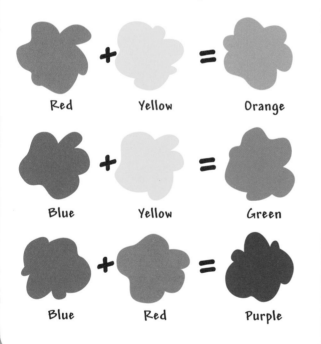

Red	+	Yellow	=	Orange
Blue	+	Yellow	=	Green
Blue	+	Red	=	Purple

Red
Bold red catches your eye. We use it on "Stop" signs and "Danger!" warnings to get people's attention.

Red, blue, and yellow are the only colors you can't make by mixing two other colors.

58

Green
Positive green is for "Go" on traffic lights. It makes us think of spring, growth, and the natural world.

Tints and shades

Adding white to a color makes it lighter. We call this a **tint**. The more white you add, the lighter the tint. Adding a bit of black instead makes the color darker. We call this a **shade**. The more black you add, the darker the shade.

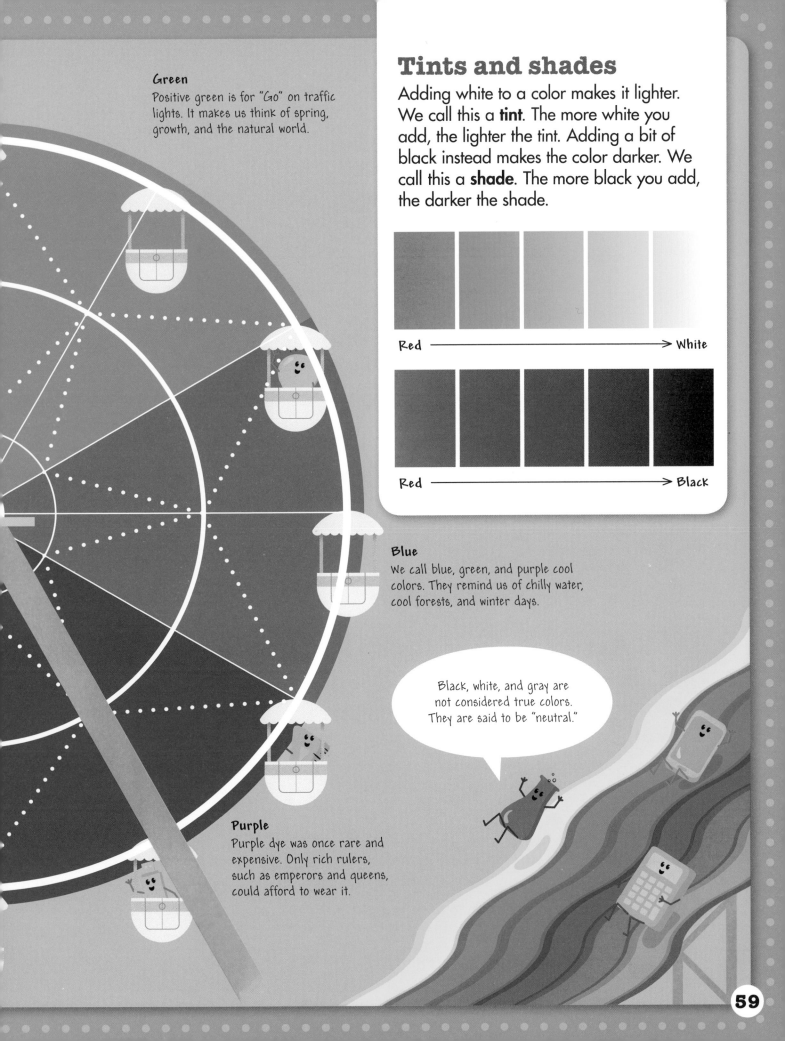

Red ⟶ White

Red ⟶ Black

Blue
We call blue, green, and purple cool colors. They remind us of chilly water, cool forests, and winter days.

Black, white, and gray are not considered true colors. They are said to be "neutral."

Purple
Purple dye was once rare and expensive. Only rich rulers, such as emperors and queens, could afford to wear it.

Materials

Materials are what we make things with. Each material has different **properties** that make it useful in different ways. Many materials can be **recycled**, which means they can be used again to make new things.

Metal
Many metals are strong, tough materials. Steel knives, forks, and spoons look shiny and are easy to clean.

Some objects can be made from different materials. A spoon can be metal, plastic, or wooden.

Plastic is made from chemicals. It doesn't break easily, and it can be formed into any shape.

Ceramic
Some bowls, plates, cups, and saucers are ceramic. They are made from soft, wet clay, which is easy to shape. The clay is then baked until it hardens.

Fabric
Fabric is made of threads woven together. The threads can come from plants or animals, or they are made from plastic. Fabric is easy to cut and sew together.

Building materials

Buildings have to last a long time. The materials construction workers use must be strong and able to resist all types of weather.

Glass windows let light in, but keep out the wind, rain, and cold.

Hard bricks make strong walls that can carry a lot of weight.

Mortar is a mixture of cement, sand, and water. It sticks bricks together.

Cardboard is made from wood pulp, too. In fact, the book you are reading comes from a tree!

Wood
Wood comes from trees. It can be cut to different lengths and hammered or screwed together to make furniture, such as this table.

Paper
Tiny chips of wood are cooked with water, until they become mushy and form a pulp. The pulp is then spread out thinly and dried to make sheets of paper.

Houses around the world

All over the world, people use different materials to build their homes, depending on what's available nearby.

Mud hut
This hut is made from mud and straw.

Log cabin
This home has wooden walls and shingles.

Igloo
An igloo is made of thick blocks of snow.

Power

Most of the electricity that comes to our homes is produced by machines called **generators**. They can be powered by fossil fuels, wind, or running water. We can also make electricity from sunlight.

Wind turbine

A wind turbine is a tall tower with propellerlike blades. As the wind blows the blades around, they spin a **shaft** (rod), which drives an electricity generator.

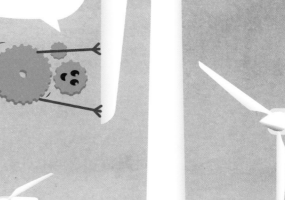

A gearbox and shaft link the propeller to the generator.

The propeller turns in the wind.

The generator produces electricity.

Fossil fuels

Coal, crude oil, and natural gas are called fossil fuels because they formed over millions of years from the remains of ancient living things. They are burned in power plants to drive generators. Burning fossil fuels releases polluting gases into the air.

Don't try this at home!

Solar farm

Electricity produced from sunlight is called **solar power**. A solar farm has lots of panels made of special materials that make electricity when the sun shines on them.

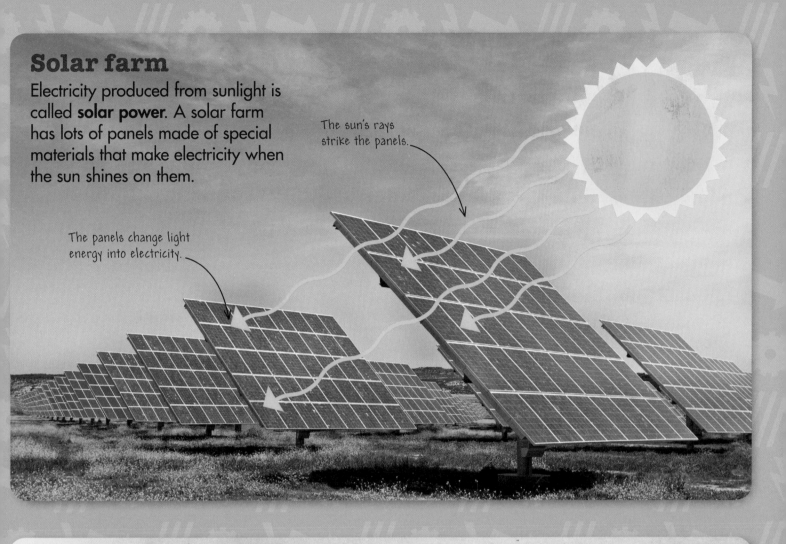

The sun's rays strike the panels.

The panels change light energy into electricity.

Hydroelectricity

Water held behind a high dam tumbles down through a tunnel in the dam wall. The water turns a set of blades called a **turbine**, which connects to a generator.

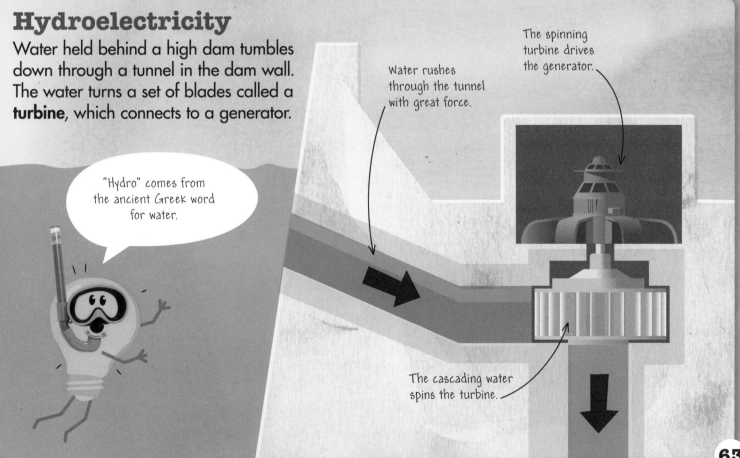

"Hydro" comes from the ancient Greek word for water.

Water rushes through the tunnel with great force.

The spinning turbine drives the generator.

The cascading water spins the turbine.

Electricity

Electricity is a type of **energy**. It powers many machines and devices, from fast trains to smart phones. For electricity to work, the things it powers must be connected by a circuit.

Circuit

A circuit is a complete loop around which electricity can **flow**. The flow of electricity is called a **current**. If there is a gap in the loop, current cannot flow. A circuit must include a source of electricity, such as a **battery**.

A circuit may include parts such as a switch, bulb, buzzer, or motor. These parts are called **components**.

Bulb
This bulb glows with light when electricity flows through it. The bulb will only light up if it is part of an electric circuit.

Battery
Inside a battery are **chemicals** that make electricity. Wires must be connected to each end of the battery for current to flow.

Battery basics

A battery has two ends called **terminals**— one is negative (-) and the other is positive (+). When wires are connected to the terminals, electricity flows out of the battery, zooms around the circuit, and then returns to the battery.

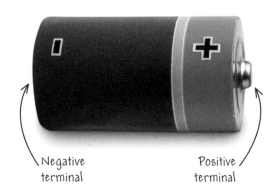

Negative terminal

Positive terminal

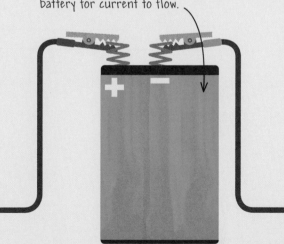

The electricity that comes to your home is dangerously powerful. **Never** put your fingers in electrical sockets.

Conductors

A material that electricity can flow through easily is called a **conductor**. Metals are good conductors. Water also conducts electricity well, so make sure you do not touch electrical objects with wet hands—stay safe!

Copper wire
Copper is a type of metal, and it is a very good conductor. Copper wire is often used to connect electrical components in a circuit.

Graphite
Pencil "lead" is made of a material called graphite. Crumbly graphite is not a metal, but it does conduct electricity.

Wires
The current flows through a loop made of metal wires.

Switch
Putting a switch in a circuit lets you control the current. With a switch, you can turn the flow of electricity on or off.

Insulators

Materials that block the flow of electric current are known as **insulators**. Good insulators include rubber, wood, wool, glass, air, and plastic. Insulators are used to keep electrical equipment safe.

Rubber
Electricians often wear rubber gloves and boots when working. Rubber does not conduct electricity, so it stops them from getting electric shocks.

Plastic
Plastics are used to coat wires and cables to stop electricity from leaking out. They are also used to make electrical plugs and sockets.

Switch control

A switch is something that can break the loop of an electric circuit. Turning the switch off opens a gap in the loop. Turning the switch on closes the gap.

Switch off
The loop is broken. Electricity cannot travel across the gap in the circuit, so the bulb will not light up.

Switch on
The loop is complete. With the gap closed, electricity flows around the circuit and the bulb shines.

65

Transportation

People are always on the move. Every day we use cars, bikes, trains, and buses to **transport** us, or get us from place to place.

Some roads have special lanes that only buses can use, so they do not get stuck in traffic jams.

Cars
Some cars are two-seaters, while others can fit in lots of people. Most car engines run on gas or diesel, but burning these fuels gives off polluting gases.

Motorcycles
Two wheels and an engine can get you places fast! Some motorcycless are for long road trips, but this scooter is for whizzing through city traffic.

Bus

Buses have seats for lots of people, and they can be a cheap way to travel. Some buses, called double-deckers, have two levels of seats linked by stairs.

Electric cars

Some cars have battery-powered motors. The battery is charged by plugging it into an electrical socket. Electric cars do not splutter out polluting exhaust fumes.

Make sure you wear a helmet every time you ride your bike!

Bicycles

Pedal bikes don't need fuel—just muscle power! They're a great way of staying in shape while traveling.

Subway trains

City subway trains rumble through underground tunnels, or clatter over tracks. They often carry hundreds of passengers at a time.

Computers

A computer is a machine that lets you work with information, such as words, pictures, or videos. We call computer information **data**. Instructions, called programs, tell the computer what to do.

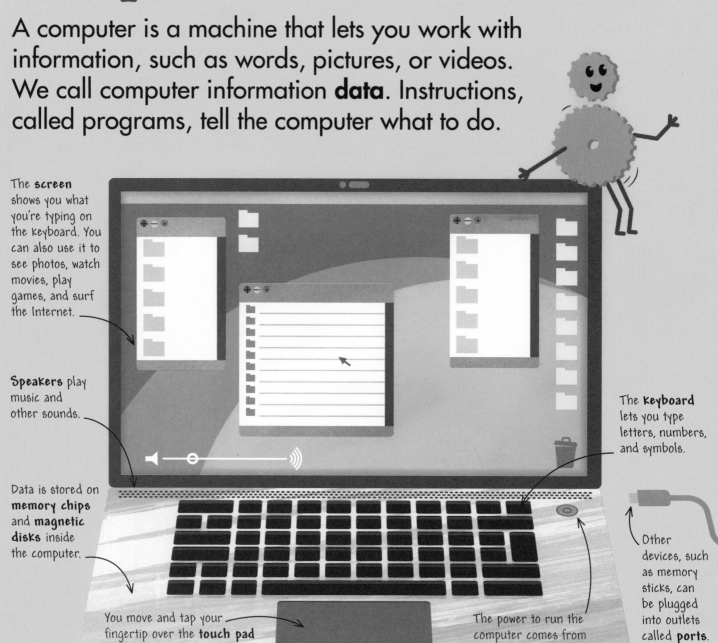

The **screen** shows you what you're typing on the keyboard. You can also use it to see photos, watch movies, play games, and surf the Internet.

Speakers play music and other sounds.

Data is stored on **memory chips** and **magnetic disks** inside the computer.

You move and tap your fingertip over the **touch pad** to select things on the screen.

The **keyboard** lets you type letters, numbers, and symbols.

Other devices, such as memory sticks, can be plugged into outlets called **ports**.

The power to run the computer comes from a built-in **battery**.

Storing data

Computer data needs to be saved so that it can be shared and used again. The way data is stored has changed a lot since the early days of computers.

Punched tape
In the 1950s, computers stored data as holes punched into tape.

Floppy disk
From the 1970s, data was stored as magnetic patterns on a thin disk.

CD (compact disc)
Data is stored as patterns of tiny pits in the surface of the disc.

The Internet

The Internet is a huge web of connected computers across the world. It has many uses, such as letting us send messages and photos instantly to anyone, anywhere with Internet access!

Shopping

Instead of going to the store to buy things, you can shop over the Internet.

Wi-Fi

Wi-Fi lets your computer or phone connect to the Internet without any wires or cables.

More than 4 billion people throughout the world use the Internet!

Email

This is a way of sending messages to people across the Internet.

Search engine

A search engine helps you find information on the Internet.

DVD (digital video disc)

DVDs have more storage space than CDs, so they are used to hold movies.

Memory stick

A memory stick is much smaller than a DVD, but it can hold much more data.

Cloud storage

Now we can store data on the Internet, so we don't need physical storage devices.

Cities

Big cities are crammed full of places for people to live, work, and enjoy themselves. Buildings in the city center are often very tall and tightly packed together to save space.

Factories
Factories make the things we use in our daily lives. They are often noisy places, since they are full of big machines.

Homes
This building has lots of homes, which are called apartments. They are arranged on different floors. You reach them by stairs or elevators.

Construction

Workers stand on a frame with platforms, called **scaffolding**, while they build a new building.

Heavy lifter
Big **cranes** are needed to lift building materials to the top of the scaffolding.

Museums
In museums. people can see famous paintings, dinosaur fossils, scientific displays, and other important objects from history.

Stores and more
Some department stores are really huge and can be the size of an entire city block. There are also malls and plenty of smaller stores.

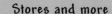

Skyscrapers
Extremely tall buildings are called **skyscrapers**. The tallest ones have more than 100 floors, or **stories**. Skyscrapers are often used as hotels or offices.

Many skyscrapers are made of steel, concrete, and glass.

Office buildings
Many people travel to city centers each day to work in offices. In most office buildings, people sit at desks and work on computers.

The world's tallest building is the Burj Khalifa in Dubai, United Arab Emirates. It has 163 floors!

Eye-catching buildings

A lot of buildings can look like boxes. But there are plenty of others with unusual shapes—some weird, and some wonderful!

The Eiffel Tower in Paris, France
This is a rocket-shaped iron tower.

The Shard in London, UK
This is a needlelike skyscraper.

Taj Mahal in Agra, India
This building has beautiful white domes.

Bridges

If you find yourself facing a big gap you can't cross—you need to build a bridge! The first bridges were made of wood or stone. Today, most bridges are made of steel and concrete.

The Golden Gate Bridge in San Francisco is 8,981 ft (2,737 m) long!

The road hangs from thick metal cables.

The cables are draped over high towers.

The road is made of strong concrete.

Suspension bridge

The towers are fixed firmly into the ground or riverbed.

Bridge types

There are several different types of bridge. When deciding what type to build, **engineers** think about whether the bridge will need to carry heavy or light loads, and whether it will be short or long.

Arch
This bridge is an arch, with each end fixed to the ground. Several arches with a road on top are used to cross a wide gap.

Truss
A truss bridge has a metal frame made of triangles, which are the strongest shapes. It can carry heavy loads.

Beam
A straight part, called the beam, rests on supports at each end. Long beam bridges also have supports in the middle.

Tunnels

In busy cities, tunnels beneath the crowded streets are often the quickest way to get around. Other tunnels allow vehicles and trains to go right through mountains and under rivers and seas.

There are tunnels for walkers, cyclists, cars, trains, water, electricity cables, phone lines, and even sewage!

Digging a tunnel
In the past, tunnels had to be dug by hand. Now we have machines to help!

The tunnel is lined with concrete.

The machine pushes the cutting wheel forward.

The wheel spins and has sharp cutting teeth.

A conveyor belt carries away soil and rock.

Tunnel-boring machine

This machine is like a mechanical mole— it **bores**, or digs, tunnels underground. It creeps forward slowly as the wheel at the front cuts away the soil and rock. As it moves, it lines the tunnel with concrete.

Planes and rockets

Aerospace engineers design planes, helicopters, and rockets. They need to know how to get aircraft off the ground, how to control them when they're flying, and how to bring them safely back down again.

Air rushing over the wings creates a lifting force that pulls the plane up.

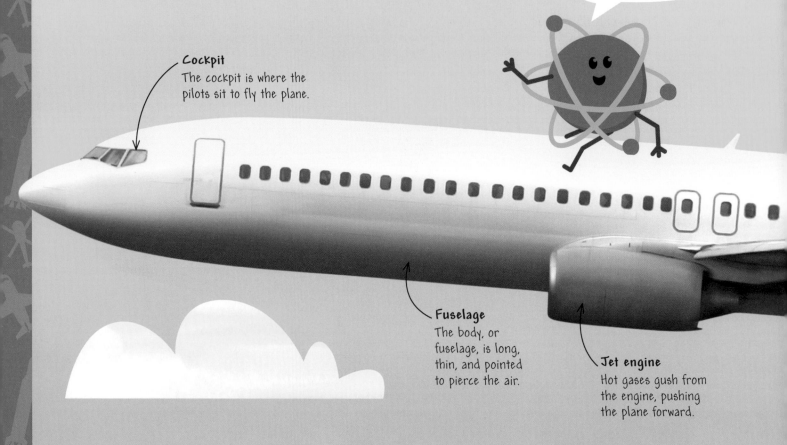

Cockpit
The cockpit is where the pilots sit to fly the plane.

Fuselage
The body, or fuselage, is long, thin, and pointed to pierce the air.

Jet engine
Hot gases gush from the engine, pushing the plane forward.

In space

Rockets lift satellites into orbit and carry astronauts up to the International Space Station. They also set robot space probes on their way to explore planets and moons.

Rockets burn LOTS of fuel at blastoff!

Space probes send information back to Earth.

Most planes are made of a strong, lightweight metal called **aluminum**.

Planes explained

A jet plane needs more than engines to fly. Wings lift the plane into the sky, and the ailerons and rudder help to steer it.

Rudder
The rudder steers the plane, turning it left or right.

Wings
The wings point backward, which helps them move through the air.

Windows
The windows are made of very tough, clear plastic.

Ailerons
These flaps tilt the wings, which helps the plane turn.

Elevator
Two elevators, one on each side, make the plane climb or descend.

Propellers and rotors

Some planes have propellers, which pull the plane through the air as they spin. Helicopter and drone rotors work in a similar way. They pull the craft up, then tilt to move it forward.

Propeller plane

Helicopter

Drone

Glossary

chemicals
Substances that make up the world

classify
When scientists sort living things into categories

climate
Weather patterns for a particular area

current
Flow of electricity through a circuit

data
Information such as words and pictures

dimension
Type of measurement, such as length, width or height

dye
Substance used to change the color of something, either temporarily or permanently

energy
Energy is what makes things happen. There are different forms of energy, such as light, heat, sound, and electricity

equilateral triangle
Triangle with three sides of equal length

fuel
Substance that releases heat when it is burned

generator
Machine that changes movement, such as that of wind, into electrical energy

gravity
Force that pulls objects toward each other

habitat
Area where plants and animals live together and find all the things they need to survive

hibernation
When animals rest in a warm place all winter to survive the cold

imperial
System of measurement that uses units such as pints, inches, and ounces

magnetism
Invisible force that allows magnets to attract other magnetic objects

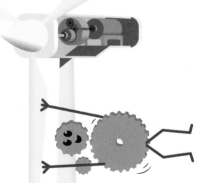

metamorphosis
Process of change many insects go through. For example, when a caterpillar changes into a butterfly

metric
System of measurement that uses units such as liters, centimeters, and grams

microbe
Any living creature too small to see without a microscope

nerves
Cells that send signals to the brain so it can figure out what's going on

nutrients
Substances found in food that help us grow

organs
Body parts that are designed for specific jobs. The heart is an example of an organ

ovule
Flower part needed to form new seeds

particles
Extremely small pieces of matter. Solids, liquids, and gases are made up of particles

photosynthesis
Process that green plants use to make food from the sun's energy

pollution
Waste that has been dumped in water, on land, or in the air

property
Something about a material that can be described and measured, such as its strength or softness

satellite
An object that moves around a planet. The Moon is a natural satellite of Earth. Satellites can also be machines that are sent into space to collect scientific information as they circle Earth

senses
Things that make you aware of the world. The five senses are sight, hearing, smell, taste, and touch

species
Types of plants and animals

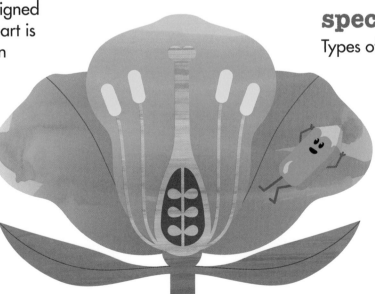

Index

A

adults 24
ailerons 75
air resistance 51
aircraft 74–75
amphibians 18, 25
analog clocks 44
animal groups 18–19
animals 26, 28, 29, 31
antennae 21
apex predators 22
arch bridges 72
art 7
asteroids 41
astronomers 41
atmosphere 36
attraction 53
axis, Earth's 38

B

babies 24
balanced forces 50
batteries 64, 67
beam bridges 72
bicycles 67
birds 18
body parts, insect 20
bones 9
boring machines 73
brain 9
brass instruments 57
bread 13
bridges 72
building materials 61
buildings 71
bulbs, light 64
burgers 12–13
buses 67

C

calendar 45
carbohydrates 11
carbon dioxide 15, 28
carnivores 22, 23
carpels 16
cars 66, 67
ceramics 60
Ceres 41
children 24
circuits, electrical 64–65
cities 70–71, 73
cleanliness 10
climates 26
clocks 44
clouds 32
cockpits 74
color 58–59
computers 68–69
condensation 48
conductors 65
conservation 29, 33
construction 70
crustaceans 19
current, electrical 64
cycling 29, 67

D

dairy products 11, 13
data storage 68–69
days 45
deciduous trees 15
decomposers 22, 23
deposition 48
deserts 27
diet 11
digital clocks 44
dinosaurs 35
drones 75
dry season 31
dwarf planets 41

E

ears 8, 56
Earth 30, 36, 38, 40
echoes 56
eclipses, solar 39
eggs 25
electric cars 67
electricity 62, 63, 64–65
elevators 75
email 69
embryos 17
endoskeleton 21
energy conservation 29
engineering 7
environment 28–29
evaporation 32, 49
evergreen trees 14
exercise 11
exoskeleton 21

F

fabrics 60
factories 28, 70
fall 31
farming 12, 13
fats 11
fish 18
flowers 16, 54
food 11, 12–13, 17
food chains 22–23
forces 50–51, 74
forests 26
fossil fuels 62
fossils 35
freezing 49
friction 51
frogs 25
fruits and vegetables 11, 12, 13
fuselages 74

G

gases 48
generators 62
germs 10
glaciers 33
global warming 29
grasslands 26

gravity 37, 38, 51
growth 24

H

habitats 22, 26–27, 29, 31
harmony 57
health 10–11
hearing 8
heart 9
helicopters 75
herbivores 22, 23
hibernation 31
homes 61, 70
hours 44
houses 61
human body 8–9
human life cycle 24
hydroelectricity 63

I

ice 29, 32, 33, 49
igneous rocks 34
insects 17, 19, 20–21
insulators 65
International Space Station 74
Internet 69
invertebrates 19

JK

jet engines 74, 75
Jupiter 40, 41
keyboards 57
kinetic energy 50

L

lakes 32
leaves 14, 15, 17
legs, insect 21
length 46
life cycles 24–25
life on Earth 36

life on Earth 36
lift 74
light 39, 54–55
liquids 48, 49

M
machinery, farm 13
magnetic fields 52, 53
magnets 52–53
mammals 18
Mars 40, 41
materials, properties of 60–61
math 7
matter 48–49
measuring 46–47
meat 12
melody 57
melting 29, 49
Mercury 40
metals 60
metamorphic rocks 34
metamorphosis 25
minerals 34
minutes 44
mollusks 19
months 45
moon 37, 39
motion 50–51
motorcycles 66
mountains 26
muscles 9, 11
museums 70
music 57

NO
Neptune 40, 41
nerves 8
oceans 27, 32, 37, 73
office buildings 71
omnivores 22, 23
online safety 69
orbits 30, 37
ovules 16
oxygen 15, 36

P
paleontologists 35
paper 60
particles 48, 49

patterns 42
percussion 57
photosynthesis 15, 22
planes 74–75
planets 40–41
plants 14–17, 22, 26, 28, 29
plastic 28
Pluto 41
polar regions 27, 29
poles, magnetic 52, 53
pollen 16
pollination 16, 17
pollution 28, 66, 67
power 62–63
predators 22
prey 23
primary colors 58
processed food 12
propellers 75
properties 60
protein 11
pull 51
push 50

R
rain 32
rays 54
recycling 29
reflective symmetry 43
reptiles 18
repulsion 53
rivers 28, 32, 33, 73
robotic probes 74
rockets 50, 74
rocks 34, 36, 37
roots 17
rotational symmetry 43
rotors 75
rudders 75
rulers 46

S
satellites 74
Saturn 40
scaffolding 70
scales 47
science 6
search engines 69
seasons 30–31

secondary colors 58
seconds 44
sedimentary rocks 34
seeds 17
senses 8, 20
sequences 42
shades 59
shadows 55
shapes 42, 43
shopping 69, 70
sight 8
skeletons 9, 21
skyscrapers 71
sleep 10
smell 8
soil 34, 36
solar power 63
solar system 40
solids 48, 49
sound 56–57
sound waves 56
space 74
spiders 19
spring 30
stamens 16
states of matter 48–49
steam 48
string instruments 57
sublimation 49
subway trains 67
summer 31
sun 30, 32, 36, 37, 38–39, 63
sunlight 15, 22, 30, 39, 62
switches 65
symmetry 43

T
tadpoles 25
taste 8
technology 6
teenagers 24
teeth 9, 10
temperature 46, 48
terminals 64
tessellation 42
thermometers 46
thorax 20, 21
thrust 50

tides 37
time 44–45
tints 59
toddlers 24
touch 8
transportation 66–67
trees 14–15, 28, 29
tropical environments 31
trunks, tree 14
truss bridges 72
tunnels 73
turbines 62, 63

UV
ultraviolet light 54
Uranus 40
Venus 40
vertebrates 18
vibrations 56, 57
volume 47

W
waste 28
water 15, 17, 28, 29, 32–33, 36, 48–49, 56
water cycle 32
water vapor 32, 48
wavelengths 55
weather 30, 31
weight 47
wet season 31
Wi-Fi 69
wind 17
wind turbines 62
wings 21, 75
winter 30
wires 65
wood 60
woodwind 57
worms 19

Y
years 45

Acknowledgments

DK would like to thank the following:
Lizzie Davey and Satu Fox for additional
editorial; Caroline Hunt for proofreading;
and Helen Peters for the index.

The publisher would like to thank the following for their
kind permission to reproduce their photographs:

(Key: a-above; b-below/bottom; c-center; f-far; l-left;
r-right; t-top)

1 Dreamstime.com: Shakila Malavige. 5 123RF.com: peterwaters
(cr); PAN XUNBIN (c). 9 123RF.com: tribalium123 (ca). Dorling
Kindersley: Stephen Oliver (cr). Dreamstime.com: Georgii Dolgykh
/ Gdolgikh (fcr). 10 Dreamstime.com: Piotr Marcinski (bc). 12
Dreamstime.com: Muriel Lasure (cb). 13 Dorling Kindersley:
Westcombe Dairy / Gary Ombler (c). Dreamstime.com: Stockr
(crb); Yuriyzhuravov (cb); Rudmer Zwerver (cra). 14 Dreamstime.
com: Denys Kurylow (Tree images). 15 123RF.com: bmf2218 (cra).
Dorling Kindersley: Westonbirt, The National Arboretum (cr).
Dreamstime.com: Selensergen (l/Tree images). 16 Getty Images:
Photodisc / Frank Krahmer (cra). 17 iStockphoto.com: t_kimura
(b). 18 123RF.com: Eric Isselee (crb). Dreamstime.com: Isselee
(cl); Menno67 (ca); Maria Itina (cr); Sneekerp (bl). 19 123RF.com:
Richard E Leighton Jr (cla). Dorling Kindersley: Linda Pitkin (clb);
Weymouth Sea Life Centre (br). Dreamstime.com: Eric Isselee
(cl). 20 Dorling Kindersley: Forrest L. Mitchell / James Laswel
clb); Natural History Museum, London (clb/Longhorn beetle).
Dreamstime.com: Andrey Burmakin / Andreyuu (clb/Green shield
bug); Marcouliana (cl). 21 123RF.com: peterwaters (tc/Bee); PAN
XUNBIN (tc/scarab may beetle). Dreamstime.com: Isselee (tc). 22
Dreamstime.com: Neirfy (c). 23 Dorling Kindersley: Jerry Young
(tl). Dreamstime.com: Iakov Filimonov (tc); Isselee (tl/Chimpanzee,
clb); Sarayut Thaneerat (tr). 26 123RF.com: atosan (b). Dreamstime.
com: Menno67 (cra, tr); Daria Rybakova / Podarenka (cr).
27 123RF.com: Bonzami Emmanuelle / cynoclub (clb); ferli (ca);
lurin (cl). Dorling Kindersley: Jerry Young (bc). Dreamstime.com:
Outdoorsman (c). 30 123RF.com: Andrew Mayovskyy / jojjik (crb).
Dreamstime.com: Stevieuk (cra). 31 123RF.com: PaylessImages
(cla). Dreamstime.com: Fesus Robert (clb). iStockphoto.com: Joel
Carillet (ca). 32 123RF.com: David Wingate (bc). iStockphoto.com:
VickySP (br). 33 123RF.com: Anton Starikov / coprid
(cb). Dreamstime.com: Achim Baqué (bc); Ilya Genkin
/ Igenkin (tl); Ruslan Gilmanshin (cra). iStockphoto.
com: JohnnyLye (bl). 35 123RF.com: Alfredo
González Sanz (bl). Dorling
Kindersley: Dorset Dinosaur
Museum (br); Natural History
Museum, London (crb). 36 123RF.com: andreykuzmin (cra/Soil);
Mykola Mazuryk (cra); David Wingate (ca/Water). Alamy Stock
Photo: Dennis Hallinan (ca). 38 Dreamstime.com: Christos
Georghiou (cl). Getty Images: Photographer's Choice / Tom Walker
(br). 40 Dreamstime.com: Nerthuz (ca). 41 NASA: JPL-Caltech,
UCLA, MPS,DLR,IDA (crb). 42 Dreamstime.com: Andreykuzmin
(br). 43 Alamy Stock Photo: Ted Kinsman (cra). 46 123RF.com:
sergofoto (tr). 50 Dreamstime.com: Konstantin Shaklein /
3dsculptor (c); Whilerests (cr). 51 123RF.com: Stanislav Pepeliaev
(crb). 52 Dreamstime.com: Dan Van Den Broeke / Dvande (bc).
54 123RF.com: fotana (cla); stillfx (cl). Dreamstime.com: Svetlana
Foote (cra). 56 Alamy Stock Photo: Jan Wlodarczyk (bc).
Dreamstime.com: Corey A. Ford / Coreyford (br). 61 123RF.com:
ivan kmit / smit (crb). Dreamstime.com: Aleksandr Bognat (cl).
Getty Images: The Image Bank / Michael Wildsmith (cl/brick).
iStockphoto.com: DNY59 (c); RTimages (cla). 62 iStockphoto.com:
AFransen (bl). 63 Dreamstime.com: Broker (ca). 65 123RF.com:
phive2015 (bc). Dreamstime.com: Bjørn Hovdal / Bear66 (cb);
Christophe Testi (cra). 66 123RF.com: Vladimir Kramin (cl). 66-67
Dreamstime.com: Nerthuz (b). iStockphoto.com: RTimages (t). 67
123RF.com: nerthuz (cra). Dorling Kindersley: Stuart's Bikes (cb).
68 123RF.com: alisali (bc); Elnur Amikishiyev / elnur (br). 69
Dreamstime.com: Marekp (bc). 70 Alamy Stock Photo: Greg
Balfour Evans (bl). 71 123RF.com: Maria Wachala (cra). Alamy
Stock Photo: Anna Stowe (crb). Dreamstime.com: Arenaphotouk
(br). 72 Dreamstime.com: Lefteris Papaulakis (cb); Yudesign (tr);
T.w. Van Urk (crb). 73 Getty Images: Science & Society Picture
Library (bc). 74 iStockphoto.com: 3DSculptor (bc). 74-75 123RF.
com: Olga Serdyuk (c). 75 Dreamstime.com: Andylid (bc/
Helicopter); Maria Feklistova (bc); Mihocphoto (br)

Cover images: *Front:* 123RF.com: Eric Isselee br/ (frog); Dorling
Kindersley: Stuart's Bikes cra; Dreamstime.com: Broker cra/
(solar power plant), Maria Itina crb, Shakila Malavige, Menno67
crb/eagle, Sneekerp br, Yudesign cl; *Back:* 123RF.com: givaga /
Sergii Kolesnyk bc; Dreamstime.com: Shakila Malavige; *Spine:*
123RF.com: goodluz t

All other images © Dorling Kindersley
For further information see: www.dkimages.com